ACHIEVING EMOTIONAL CONTROL

A GUIDE FOR DEALING WITH AND OVERCOMING NEGATIVE EMOTIONS

DERRICK SMITH

CONTENTS

INTRODUCTION

I was 12 when I initially began to feel futile and deserted. I kept a diary, which I wrote in each day. I in some cases composed that I wanted to be alive, so I wouldn't hurt so a lot. At the point when I was 15, I had a breakdown one day at school. I was taken to the emergency clinic, where I was focused on by individuals who needed to help me. I was placed taking drugs, which didn't help that much, however, I before long started the excursion to become 'me' once more, albeit I didn't know what my identity was. Because of being harassed, I exited the school. I chose to begin partaking in my nearby local area; thus, I started a year of the traineeship. In any case, I found figuring out how to adapt both at work and home truly hard.

In this book, you will figure out how to comprehend and deal with your feelings - your own and others - in a manner that is useful and can make a genuine, good distinction in your life.

CHAPTER 1

RECOGNIZING YOUR EMOTIONS

You've probably heard that emotion is an important factor in predicting success in most, if not all, fields. Self-awareness—the capacity to feel, name, and not be overwhelmed by emotions—is the foundation of emotions.

However, if you believe you are lacking in emotional awareness, how can you improve it?

The concept of "emotion" encompasses several aspects of experience and is quite broad and even ambiguous:

I refer to feelings as the perception or experience of bodily states. For instance, fear makes your heart race.

Patterns of thought and thinking, specifically internal dialogue. For instance, when you are angry, you may consider taking revenge.

There are also different ways of thinking: depression causes slow, repetitive thinking.

Impulses and urges to act: When you're angry, you might want to yell or even hit someone.

Attention: You tend to focus in particular ways and on particular things; for instance, when you're anxious, you tend to narrow your focus to what could go wrong.

CHAPTER 2

UNDERSTANDING HOW EMOTIONS ARE DEVELOPED

Understanding what feelings and emotions are, how and why they occur, recognizing one's feelings as well as those of others, and developing effective strategies for managing those feelings are all part of emotional development. Joy, rage, sadness, and fear are the first feelings that babies can identify. More complex emotions like shyness, surprise, elation, embarrassment, shame, guilt, pride, and empathy emerge as children's sense of self develops. Children and adolescents are still learning to identify emotions, understand why they occur, and manage them appropriately.

Let's concentrate on their three main components—the subjective experience, the physiological response, and the behavioural response—to better comprehend emotions.

Subjective Experience

Experts believe that there are several fundamental, universal emotions that people of all backgrounds and cultures experience, but researchers also believe that emotional experience can be highly subjective. Take, for example, rage. Is rage universal? Your own experience could be anything from mild irritation to blinding rage.

Although we commonly refer to feelings as "angry," "sad," or "happy," your own experience of these feelings may be much more complex and, as a result, subjective.

Additionally, we don't always experience each emotion in its purest form. It's common for us to experience mixed feelings about various life events or circumstances. You may feel both excited and nervous about starting a new job. A wide range of feelings, from joy to anxiety, can accompany getting married or having a child. You might experience all of these feelings at once, or you might feel them one after the other.

Physiological Response

If you've ever felt your heart beat faster or your stomach churn from anxiety, you know that emotions can also cause strong physiological responses.

The sympathetic nervous system, which is a part of the autonomic nervous system, controls many of the physiological responses you experience during an emotion, like sweaty palms and a racing heartbeat.

Blood flow and digestion are examples of involuntary body responses that are controlled by the autonomic nervous system. The body's fight-or-flight responses are controlled by the sympathetic nervous system. These responses automatically prepare your body for either fleeing or confronting a threat head-on.

More recent research has focused on the brain's role in emotions, whereas earlier studies of the physiology of emotion tended to concentrate on these autonomic responses. The amygdala, which is part of the limbic system and is involved in emotion and fear, in particular, has been shown to play a significant role in brain scans.

Motivational states like hunger and thirst, as well as memory and emotion, have been linked to the amygdala itself, a tiny almond-shaped structure. The amygdala is activated when people are shown threatening images, according to brain imaging research. The fear response has also been shown to be impaired by damage to the amygdala.

Behavioural Response

The final aspect—the actual expression of emotion—may be one that you are most familiar with. Emotional intelligence, as psychologists refer to it, is linked to our capacity to accurately comprehend these expressions, which are a significant component of our overall body language.

According to research, many expressions are universal, such as smiling to express happiness or frowning to express sadness.

Emotional expression and interpretation are also influenced by social and cultural norms. When an authority figure is present, for instance, people in Japan have a propensity to cover up expressions of fear or disgust. While people in Japan are more likely to do so while alone, people in the United States are more likely to express negative emotions both alone and in the presence of others.

CHAPTER 3

WHAT INFLUENCES YOUR EMOTIONS

Everything from what you decide to eat for breakfast to which political candidates you choose to support is heavily influenced by your feelings.

Emotions play a crucial role, even in situations where you believe your decisions are solely based on logic and reason. It has been demonstrated that emotional intelligence, or your capacity to comprehend and control your emotions, plays a significant role in decision-making.

DO PEOPLE INFLUENCE YOUR EMOTIONS?

Do you feel influenced by other people?

Empathy enables you to comprehend the emotions of others and see things from their point of view. People's desires determine whether others can influence their emotions. Compassion and concern for the well-being of other people can be cultivated through this important social responsibility.

Empathy is something that comes naturally to everyone, but it is typically regarded more as a skill than a trait. It begins with the people who cared for you as a child and grows through a combination of your experiences and relationships. It is essential to keep in mind that genes also play a minor role in the formation of empathy.

As a consequence of this, individuals develop varying degrees of empathy as adults.

Empaths are people whose empathy is so strong that they seem to understand other people's feelings.

If you are an empath, you might find that you take in the feelings of others. You get caught up in their happiness when they are happy.

You also carry the emotional burden of their sadness.

First, a look at the main kinds of empathy. Knowing the different kinds of empathy can help you understand how empathy and anxiety are related.

Empathy with the mind. The capacity to comprehend the emotions of another person is referred to here. Body language and tone of voice, for instance, may provide clues about their underlying thoughts and feelings.

Emotional empathy's capacity to express one's emotions to another is the subject of this. This emotional empathy, which typically develops on its own, can cultivate compassion and inspire you to assist.

Affective empathy is typically high in empaths. You feel the emotional pain of worry and stress when people you care about are going through it. You might feel anxious and worried for them as long as they continue to struggle.

Now, let's see how we can put these feelings and empathy to good use

CHAPTER 4

EXPRESSING YOUR POSITIVE EMOTIONS

Being human necessitates the ability to experience both positive and negative emotions. Although we may use the term "negative" to describe more difficult feelings, this does not imply that those feelings are undesirable or that we should not experience them. However, the majority of people probably would rather experience a positive emotion than a negative one. You probably would rather be happy than sad or confident than insecure. The way our emotions are balanced is what matters.

Positive emotions not only counterbalance negative ones, but they also have other significant advantages.

Positive emotions affect our brains in ways that improve our awareness, attention, and memory rather than narrowing our focus as negative emotions do. They assist us in taking in more information, remembering multiple concepts at once, and comprehending how concepts relate to one another.

We are better able to learn and improve our skills when we experience positive emotions that open our minds to new possibilities. As a result, you'll do better on tests and tasks.

Positive emotions tend to make people happier, healthier, and more able to learn and get along with others.

The Value of Positive Emotions Science is revealing the importance of positive emotions. Recent research on the brain has revealed a lot to experts. Two findings can help us make better use of our positive emotions:

1. When we experience a greater proportion of positive emotions than negative ones, it is simpler to deal with challenging circumstances.

Our resilience—the emotional resources required for coping—is bolstered by positive emotions. They let us see more options for resolving problems because they broaden our awareness.

According to research, individuals perform at their highest levels when they experience at least three times as many positive emotions as negative emotions. This is due to a phenomenon known as the negativity bias.

The natural human tendency to focus more on negative emotions than on positive ones is known as the negativity bias. If you consider it, it makes sense: Emotions of negativity bring to our attention issues that may require immediate attention. Being able to tune into negative feelings can be a survival strategy.

However, the negative bias has a drawback: Even if we experienced equal amounts of positive and negative emotions that day, it can cause us to believe that a day went poorly or poorly. To tip the scales and make a day seem great, it takes at least three times as many positive emotions.

2. Every day, try to be positive. Developing routines that encourage us to feel more positive emotions can make us happier, improve our performance, and reduce our negative emotions. If we are already dealing with a lot of negative emotions like fear, sadness, anger, frustration, or stress, it is especially important to cultivate positive emotions.

It is not difficult to establish a routine of daily positivity. There are two fundamental steps:

Observe and identify your positive feelings. Begin by simply concentrating on your emotions. You can pay attention to your feelings right now, as they happen. or at the end of the day, take stock and note how you felt in various situations. For instance, you might feel loved when your mother attends your game, happy when your puppy chases you around the yard, or proud when you correctly answer a question.

You'll likely need to keep reminding yourself to pay attention to your feelings when you first start doing this. However, like any habit, it gets easier with practice.

Choose a feeling and act to make it stronger. Let's say you pick self-assurance: What gives you confidence? How can you replicate that feeling even more? You might say, "Yes, I can!" to yourself. reassurance before a test. Or on the other hand, perhaps you stand up straighter and work on strolling through the corridors in a certain manner, feeling solid and strong.

Positive emotions are good for you and make you feel good. Make time for these potent tools in your daily routine by paying attention to them. Make time in your day for joy, having fun, spending time with friends, relaxing, being thankful, and being kind. If you make these things a routine, you will unquestionably be happier!

CHAPTER 5

DIRECTING YOUR EMOTIONS IN THE RIGHT WAY

We wouldn't be worried about happiness if we didn't feel miserable, but if we keep focusing on the positive, we have no choice but to hide the negative. As a result, I want to demonstrate to you, as a supporter of all feelings, how even the most difficult feelings can illuminate and enrich our lives.

Let's think about how to put these five feelings and emotions to good use: boredom When you're bored, time stretches out, slows down, and even seems to stand still. As our sense of significance and purpose dwindles, the feeling can be accompanied by an oppressive sense of emptiness. Additionally, when we are bored, we turn to familiar sources of stimulation. However, the most fertile ground for innovation and transformation can be found in this state of emptiness. Things will remain the same as long as you keep automatically distracting yourself. You might be surprised at how creative you can be if you give yourself some breathing room.

Even if you feel uneasy, reframe boredom as a time to reflect. When we are in silence, we frequently discover what we require. If you are a frequent distractor, begin with brief periods of non-distraction and gradually progress to longer ones, like when you train for a marathon.

Regret is our mind's way of reminding us to re-evaluate our previous actions. It gives us the chance to make decisions that reflect who we are, or even the person we want to be. We may be inspired to be more courageous in the future if we make a cautious decision that results in the loss of an opportunity.

Regret also presents an excellent opportunity to test your internal dialogue. You are more likely to struggle with regret if you are prone to "should" thinking. Though telling yourself you should have known better may appear to be a good way to motivate yourself, it results in punishment. Remorse is cured by compassion, not by punishment, so use times of regret as opportunities to practice giving yourself some slack.

When you have done something that you believe is wrong and has caused harm, guilt sets in. It signifies the opportunity to either rectify a situation with someone or examine your values closely. Guilt reveals that you have violated a significant personal or moral value, giving you the chance to reconnect with those values or re-evaluate them. When guilt is dealt with in this manner, it can inspire rather than paralyse.

Envy According to Bertrand Russell, a philosopher, envy is one of the most potent negative emotions; Therefore, it is worthwhile to approach it constructively. Use the fortune of someone else as an indicator of the change you need to make in your own life rather than feeling powerless in the face of it. Envy can't see: To obscure your true vision, the Latin word for envy, Invidia, comes from invaders, which means "to look against. "But when you see envy for what it is, you can see the part of you that needs to be fed.

Shame is one of the most isolating feelings. However, we can remain constructive even in this most difficult circumstance. There is much to say about shame because it is universal. However, for the time being, shame presents an opportunity to develop your capacity for compassion and forgiveness. If you've done something that you think is embarrassing or wrong, think hard about wha you believe. Do you believe that no one should ever act foolish, stupid, or wrong? Is this attainable? Every one of us has said and done things that we regret. Do you have a bad character? Or merely human? Consider what you would tell a friend who is in a similar situation: Using this can help you access your compassionate side.

CONCLUSION

Every person who experiences emotions does so in their unique way and a variety of ways.

Although happiness is wonderful, it is fleeting. There are numerous additional aspects to us. Rather than trying to live as if it were wrong to have flaws in the first place, it is better to strive to be the best version of ourselves that we can be.

I offer my love and support to anyone who feels alone and dominated by their emotions